My Friend Pearl

by Bonita Birungi & Esther Banyenzaki

Pearl loves many things in Uganda.

Pearl is a little girl.

She is 4 years old.

How old are you?

Pearl - Age 4

Pearl lives in Uganda.
Uganda is in Africa.

where do you live?

ARCTIC
Ocean

NORTH AMERICA

EUROPE

ASIA

Atlantic
Ocean

AFRICA

Pacific
Ocean

Pacific
Ocean

SOUTH
AMERICA

Indian
Ocean

AUSTRALIA

Southern
Ocean

ANTARCTICA

AFRICA

Nimule

Yumbe

Kitgum

Maracha

Arua

Abim
District

Gulu

Mahagi

Lira

Amuria

Lake
Albert

Masindi

Uganda

Soroti

Sironko

Mbale

Kaliro

Atiri

Fort Portal

Nakibungulia

Bombo

Kasowa

Tororo

Kasese

Mityana

Kampala

Jinja

Chanjojo

Entebbe

Masaka

Lake Victoria

Mbarara

7

In the morning, Pearl washes her body.

She uses a small orange towel.

what do you use to wash?

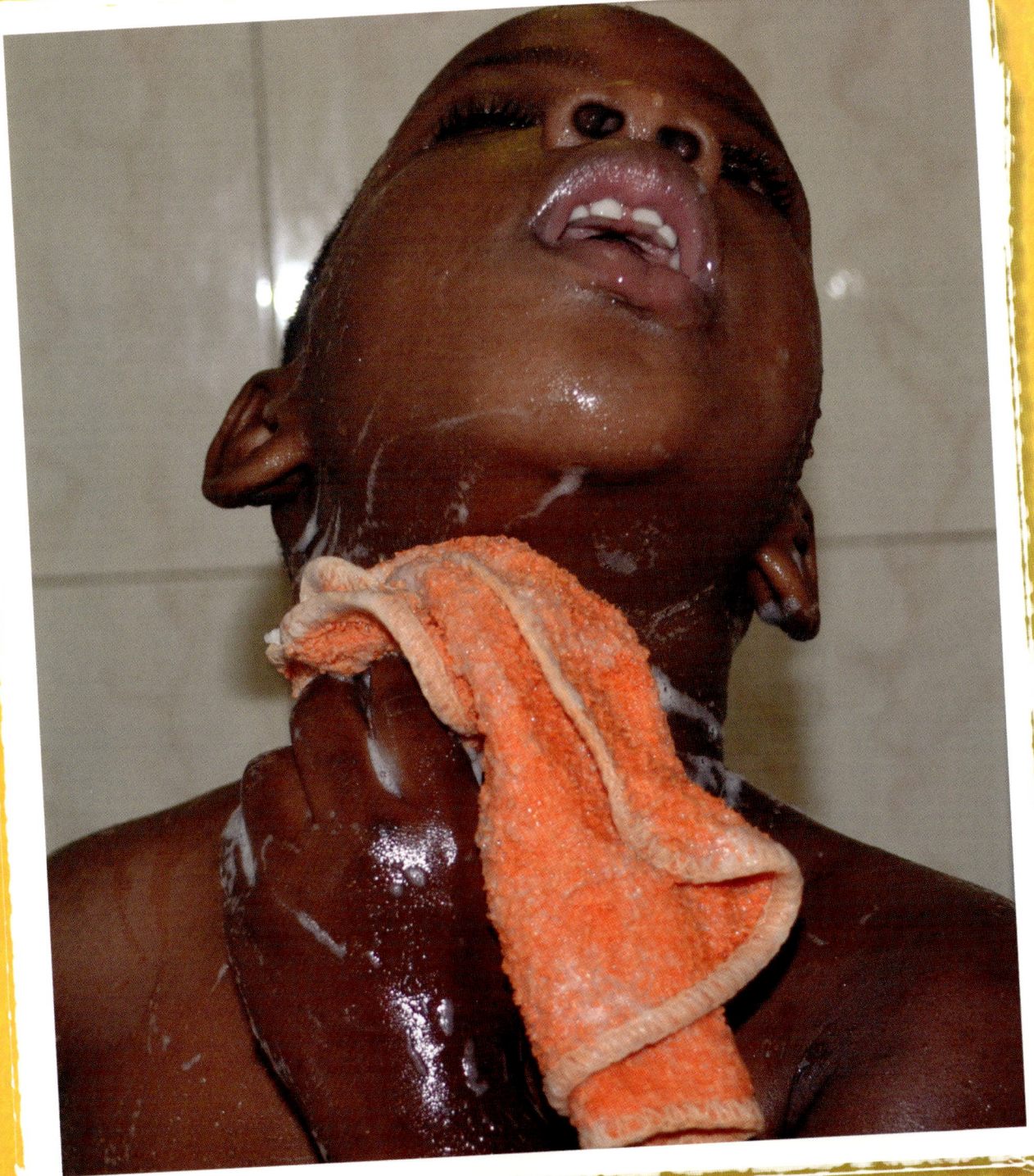

Pearl wears a uniform.

She carries a bag.

What do you
wear to school?

On her way to school,
Pearl buys juice.

She drinks it.

What do you
like to drink?

Pearl loves to learn.

She helps her teacher.

What do you
like to learn?

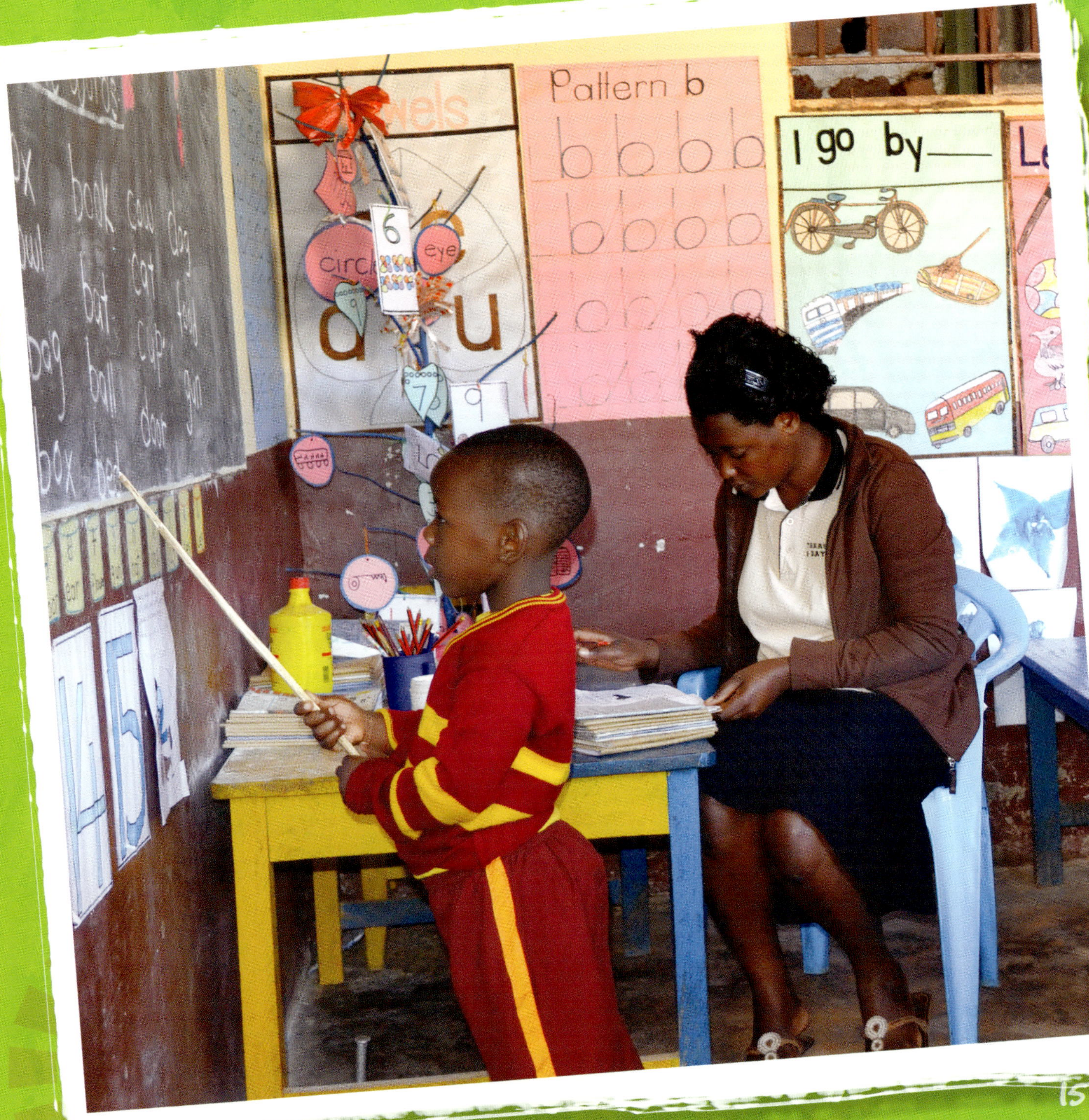
Pattern b
I go by___

Pearl plays with
her friends.

She loves her friends.

Who is your friend?

Pearl washes her hands before she eats.

When do you wash your hands?

19

Pearl is kind.

She shares a biscuit.

What do you share?

After school,
Pearl says good-bye.

She goes home to
help her family.

What do you do
after school?

Pearl helps
prepare dinner.

Pearl holds
two plantains.

How do you help
at dinner?

Pearl loves cooking.

Be careful!
The charcoal stove is hot!

What is hot
in your home?

Pearl plays
with her sister.

They love to sing.

What song
can you sing?

Pearl worked and played very hard.

She is tired.
Good night, Pearl.

where do you sleep?

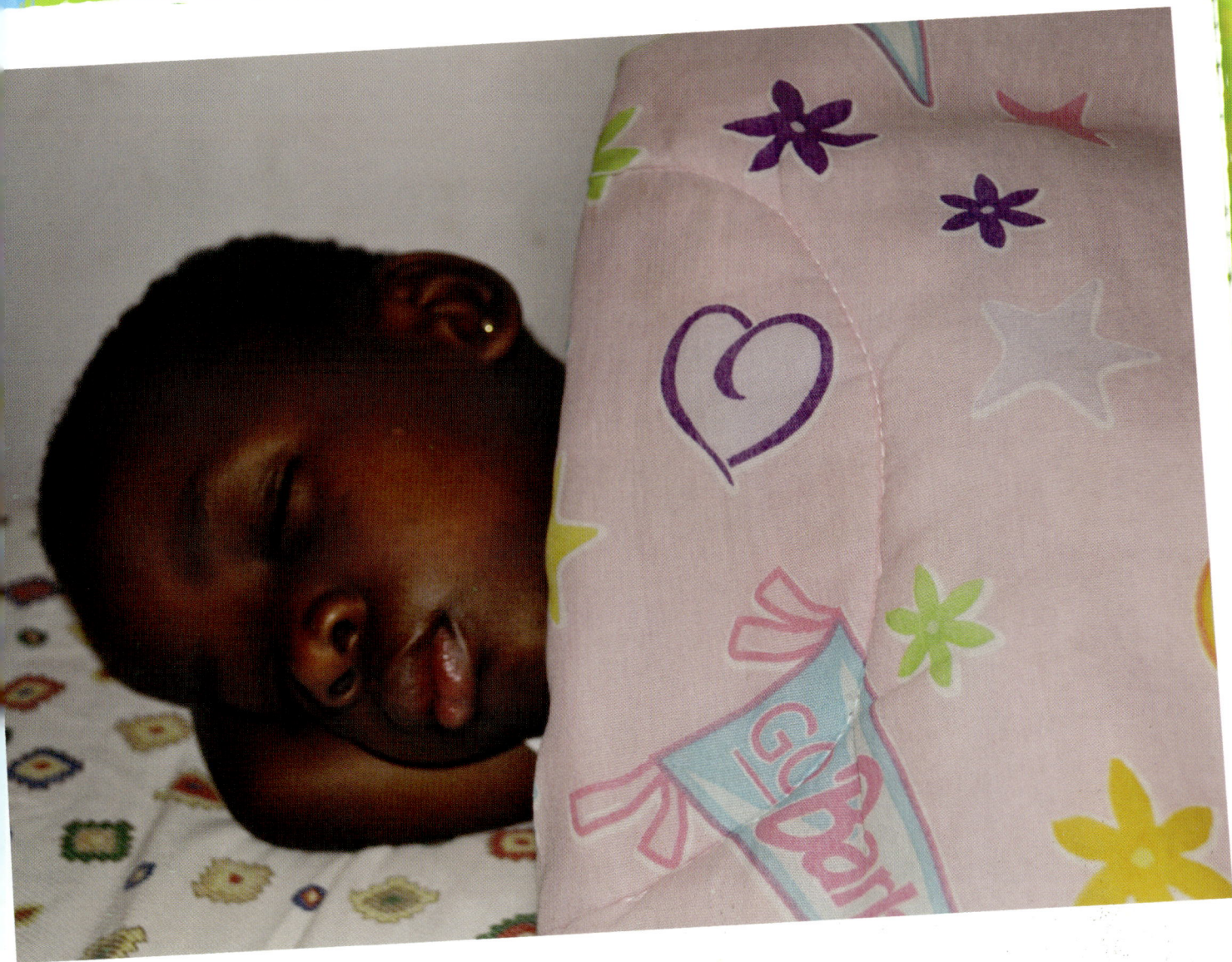

Let's Review!

Pearl loves Uganda.

She loves juice.

She loves to learn.

She loves to play.

Pearl loves to wash.

She loves her friends.

She loves to cook.

She loves her family.

What do you love?

33

fun facts about Uganda

The Crested Crane is the National Bird.

Uganda is home to the endangered Mountain Gorillas.
There are only about 786 Mountain Gorillas in the world.

On October 9th 2012, Uganda celebrated 50 years of independence.

In 1914, two of Uganda's national parks were recognized
by UNESCO as World Heritage Sites: Bwindi Impenetrable National Park
and Rwenzori Mountains National Park.

The Rwenzori Mountains are also called the 'Mountains of the Moon.'
They have glaciers, waterfalls and lakes.

Lake Victoria is the largest lake in Africa and
the second largest freshwater lake in the world.
It is shared by Uganda and Kenya.

English and Swahili are the two official languages of Uganda.

Soccer (football) is the most popular sport in Uganda.